Othello

A Shakespeare Story

RETOLD BY ANDREW MATTHEWS
ILLUSTRATED BY TONY ROSS

ORCHARD BOOKS

For Howard
A.M.

ORCHARD BOOKS
338 Euston Road, London NW1 3BH
Orchard Books Australia
Hachette Children's Books
Level 17/207 Kent St, Sydney, NSW 2000
ISBN 1 84616 180 0 (hardback)
ISBN 1 84616 184 3 (paperback)
First published in Great Britain in 2006
First paperback publication in 2007
Text © Andrew Matthews 2006
Illustrations © Tony Ross 2006
The rights of Andrew Matthews and Tony Ross to be identified as the author
and illustrator of this work have been asserted by them in accordance with
Copyright, Designs and Patents Act, 1988.
A CIP catalogue record for this book is available from the British Library.
1 3 5 7 9 10 8 6 4 2 (hardback)
1 3 5 7 9 10 8 6 4 2 (paperback)

Contents

Cast List

Othello
The Moor of Venice

Desdemona
Othello's wife

Iago
Othello's ensign

Emilia

Iago's wife

Cassio

Othello's lieutenant

Bianca

in love with Cassio

The Scene

Cyprus in the sixteenth century.

Excellent wretch! Perdition catch my soul
But I do love thee, and when I love thee not,
Chaos is come again.

Othello; III.iii.

Othello

Othello the Moor was living proof that the colour of a man's skin is less important than his courage and determination.

He had travelled widely, facing wonders and terrors in jungles and deserts. Captured and sold into slavery, he made his escape, and joined the army of the city state of Venice. His bravery and cool-headedness in battle won him steady promotion, until at last he was made a general.

And then something totally unexpected happened. Othello fell in love with beautiful young Desdemona, daughter of Brabantio, a Venetian nobleman, and his love was returned. Years of soldiering had left Othello unprepared for love, and his new emotions almost overwhelmed him.

Desdemona and Othello married in secret, knowing that Brabantio would object because of the difference in their races. When their secret was revealed, Brabantio was bitterly angry – not least at the way in which his cherished daughter

had deceived him – but he could do nothing to separate the lovers.

Instead the Venetian Senate ordered Othello to take command of a garrison on the island of Cyprus, and he took his bride with him.

As their ship left
harbour, the couple
were blissfully happy,
believing that they
were at the start of
a wonderful new
life together.

In reality, they
were sailing towards
a tragedy that
would destroy
them both.

✳ ✳ ✳

On a warm moonlit
night, Ensign Iago and
Private Roderigo were
standing guard on the
battlements of the Venetian
garrison. Roderigo was a new recruit,
young and impulsive, and Iago had given
him enough sips from a hip-flask of
brandy to make the private talkative,
and sorry for himself.

"I've loved Desdemona for years!" he groaned. "I wanted to wed her, but her father told me I wasn't good enough. After she married Othello, I joined the army and bribed a captain to order me to Cyprus so that I could be near her. Seeing her with Othello is driving me mad. What can I do?"

Tears welled up in Roderigo's eyes.

"Be patient," advised Iago. "Desdemona and Othello were quick to fall in love, and they'll tire of each other just as quickly. When that happens, you'll be among the first to know."

"How?" Roderigo asked with a drunken frown.

"My wife Emilia is Desdemona's maid," said Iago. "Desdemona confides in her, and Emilia confides in me. When I give you the word, you can use me to send her love tokens – jewels and the like. Her heart will soften, and then..."

Roderigo hiccuped. "Why would you bother to help me?"

"I hate Othello," Iago said, stony-faced. "It's not right for a Moor to command men like us. I've been a soldier half my life. I deserve to be Othello's lieutenant, but he promoted Cassio instead of me. Helping you to woo Othello's wife will be my revenge."

Iago fell silent, but his words continued in his mind.

"A wife for a wife, Moor," he thought grimly. "I don't know if those rumours about you and Emilia are true, but I know how jealousy gnaws and burns, and how quickly a doubt can become a green-eyed monster. A gentle hint that Desdemona is untrue will be enough. Jealousy will do the rest!"

* * *

The following evening, Iago called on Cassio and greeted him with a brisk salute.

"Sorry to disturb you, sir, but some townspeople have sent us a crate of wine to drink the general's health," he said. "Would you care to join us in the mess hall?"

Cassio frowned.

"I have to go on watch soon," he said.

Iago smiled encouragingly. "Not for another hour, sir. You can spare a few minutes, surely?"

"To tell you the truth, I don't have a good head for drink," admitted Cassio. "Even one cup will—"

"Don't worry, sir!" chuckled Iago. "The local wine is no stronger than grape juice."

"Very well," Cassio agreed. "But I shan't stay long."

Iago had lied about the strength of the wine, for he had secretly topped up every bottle with brandy.

In the mess hall, the men drank a toast
to Othello. Then Roderigo proposed
a toast to Desdemona, Private Montano
raised his cup to Iago, and before long
everyone was singing raucously.

Cassio gestured for silence. There was
sweat on his pale face and he peered down
his nose to keep from seeing double.

"Gentlemen, I must do my duty!" he declared. "You see how clear-headed I am, so no one can accuse me of being drunk." His mood suddenly changed and he gripped the hilt of his sword. "Does anyone dare to accuse me?" he barked.

"No one here, sir," Iago said gently.

As Cassio lurched across the hall, Iago turned to Roderigo.

"Go after him," Iago whispered. "Tell him he's too drunk to be on duty."

"After what he just said?" gasped Roderigo.

"Make him lose his temper, and lead him back here," Iago murmured. "It's part of my scheme to bring you and Desdemona together."

Roderigo hurried away.

A minute later, angry shouting was heard. Roderigo scampered into the mess hall, pursued by Cassio, who had drawn his sword.

Montano tried to restrain the lieutenant, and the two men tussled. Cassio accidentally gashed Montano's side with his sword. Soldiers bumped into each other in an attempt to separate the two. There were curses, blows, and more fighting broke out.

Iago smirked to see the uproar he had caused, but quickly straightened his face as Othello stormed into the hall.

"Stop, on pain of death!" Othello roared.

The men ceased fighting and stood with bowed heads.

"What caused this, Cassio, and why is this man bleeding?" Othello demanded.

"I can't speak, sir," said Cassio, slurring his words.

Othello turned to Iago.

"You're an honest man, Iago. Tell me the truth," he said.

"It all happened so fast, sir," said Iago. "We were all happy and singing, then Lieutenant Cassio charged in, chasing after someone or other. Montano tried to calm him down, and all at once everyone was fighting."

Othello glowered at Cassio. "Lieutenant Cassio, I discharge you from the army for being drunk on duty. Leave the garrison at dawn!"

Othello swept out. The other soldiers slunk away, leaving Iago and Cassio alone together.

Cassio buried his face in his hands.

"My career is over!" he grizzled. "I've lost my reputation."

"You'll get it back," said Iago, placing his hand on Cassio's shoulder. "You're a friend of the general's wife, aren't you?"

Cassio raised his head and nodded.

"Go to her and explain what happened – you're a young man who had too much to drink, and made a mistake you'll never make again," Iago said smoothly. "Desdemona will be sorry for you, and she'll persuade the general to reinstate you."

"Of course!" exclaimed Cassio. "Thanks, Iago. You're the wisest, most trustworthy man I've ever met."

Iago smiled.

Next day, in the shimmering heat of noon, Iago carried a satchel of dispatches to Othello's office, and waited while the general inspected them.

"Did you ask Cassio to report to you today, sir?" Iago enquired casually.

"No – why?" said Othello.

"I saw him talking to your wife earlier on."

Othello looked up from his papers. "What if he was?"

Iago squirmed, as if embarrassed. "It seemed to me they sat a little too close together, sir, and when Cassio kissed your wife's hand,  I thought his lips lingered longer than some would consider proper."

"What are you suggesting?" Othello asked sharply.

"Nothing, sir!" exclaimed Iago. "The last thing I want is to stir up trouble between man and wife. Perhaps I should have kept my mouth shut, but I'm a plain man, and I speak as I find."

"Yes," Othello said thoughtfully. "I know you do. Leave me now, Iago."

When Iago had departed, Othello stared blankly at the wall facing him.

"Iago wouldn't have mentioned seeing Cassio with Desdemona unless he suspected them of something," he thought. "Could it be? Cassio is a younger man than I am, and he is white. Does Desdemona regret marrying me?"

Othello felt sick with doubt. His world had once been solid, founded on military discipline. Since he had married, his life had seemed less certain. Though he was overjoyed to receive it, he did not understand why he had won Desdemona's love. Could he lose it just as mysteriously?

At that moment, Desdemona entered the office.

"We must talk about Cassio," she said. "I spoke to him this morning, and—"

"Not now, Desdemona," said Othello, rubbing his forehead. "I have a headache."

From her sleeve, Desdemona drew
a pretty handkerchief, embroidered
with strawberries.

"Let me bandage you with this, my
love!" she cooed.

"It's too small," said Othello.

"Look at her eyes, they're as innocent
as a child's!" he thought. "Yet they're the
same eyes that deceived her father."

Desdemona held out her hand. "Let's go to dinner."

As they left the office, neither Desdemona nor Othello noticed her handkerchief drop to the floor in the corridor outside.

A little later, Emilia and Iago strolled by. Emilia saw the handkerchief and stopped to pick it up.

"What's that?" asked Iago.

"My lady's favourite handkerchief," Emilia replied. "She worries when she misplaces it."

"Let me borrow it for a day or so, will you?" said Iago. "I'll use it to play a trick on someone."

Emilia gave
her husband the
handkerchief.

"I hope it's not
a cruel trick, like
the one played
on you when
you thought
I had been
unfaithful with
the general,"
she said.

Iago answered
with a grin,
but his mind
was weaving nets
of dark thoughts.

✳ ✳ ✳

Othello walked alone in the cool of
the evening, hoping to rid himself of the
jealous thoughts that had tortured him all
day. As he crossed the parade ground, he
met Iago.

"How are you, general?" said Iago.
"You look—"

"My mind is full of fire and poison!"
Othello burst out. "I would rather know

for sure that Desdemona is unfaithful than suffer these doubts."

Iago leaned closer. "I may have proof, sir. The other day, I saw Cassio with your wife's handkerchief – the one embroidered with strawberries."

Othello's face fell. "The first love token I ever gave her! She swore she would always keep it."

"Listen, sir," said Iago. "Your wife told Emilia that Cassio means to see you in the morning, to beg for his commission back.

I'll stop him under the window of your office, and ask him what's going on between him and your wife. If you watch from the window, you'll see how he reacts."

Othello clasped Iago to him.

"Honest Iago!" he said. "At least I know I can rely on you."

Othello could not see the icy loathing in Iago's eyes.

Cassio was anxious when he entered the garrison the next morning. He concentrated so hard on what he would say to the general that he did not notice Iago approaching, or Othello spying on him from his office window.

Iago winked at Cassio.

"A certain young lady is looking for you," Iago said.

"Bianca?" said Cassio, rolling his eyes. "She follows me everywhere! I found a lady's handkerchief in my lodgings yesterday – I've no idea where it came from – but when I gave it to Bianca, she

was as pleased as if it were a diamond ring!"

"Talking of rings, some of the men are taking bets that you'll wed her soon," Iago said.

Cassio threw back his head and laughed.

"You don't marry women like Bianca!" he exclaimed. "Not if you have any sense."

Othello's pulse pounded in his ears.

"Look at him laugh!" he thought. "He must be bragging about how eagerly Desdemona gave herself to him."

Othello was not the only one spying on Cassio. Down in the parade ground, Bianca had emerged from a shadowy doorway, and was glaring at her lover, with her hands on her hips.

"So that's what you think of me!" she seethed. "Well don't come sniffing round me again, and take this back!"

She plucked a handkerchief from the front of her dress, and flung it at Cassio. The handkerchief was so delicate that it floated as it fell, unfolding like a bird opening its wings.

Othello recognised the handkerchief as Desdemona's.

Overpowered by
shock, he uttered
a loud cry before
collapsing in
a swoon.

Iago revived
Othello a few minutes
later, and helped him
into a chair. Othello's eyes
were glassy, and his hands trembled.

"Where is Cassio?" he croaked.

"Gone," Iago said. "I came to the office as soon as I heard you call, saw you were ill and told Cassio to return to his lodgings until he was sent for. You saw me question him?"

"Yes, and I saw the handkerchief."

"The lying dog!" growled Iago. "When I think of how you trusted him, and—"

"Cassio must die!" Othello whispered.

"Leave the little sewer rat to me, sir," urged Iago. "What will you say to your wife?"

"My wife?" Othello exclaimed. "My wife!" He clenched his shaking hands into fists.

"Oh, this is sweet!" gloated Iago. "Tonight I'll get Roderigo drunk enough to believe anything, and convince him that he has to kill Cassio to win Desdemona.

We'll wait in the alley near the inn where
Cassio dines, and when he appears,
Roderigo will run him through. All
I'll have to do then is slip my dagger
between Roderigo's ribs, and no one will
know that I had anything to do with
Cassio's murder!"

Desdemona had just finished saying her prayers when Othello entered the bedroom that night. She went to kiss her husband, but stopped when she saw the grimness in his eyes.

"What's wrong, my love?" she asked. "Have I done something to offend you?"

"Where is the handkerchief I gave you as my love token?" said Othello.

Reluctant to admit
that she had lost
the handkerchief,
Desdemona frowned.
"Let me see...where
can I have left it?"
Othello seized her
by the shoulders.
"You left it in Cassio's
hands when you
took him as your
lover!" he declared.

Desdemona
stared in disbelief.
"Are you mad?" she
cried. "What are
you saying? Cassio
is my friend,
nothing more."

49

"No more lies!" bellowed Othello.
"You have broken your wedding vows,
and now you must die!"

He hurled Desdemona onto the bed,
and pressed a pillow over her face.

A shadow seemed to fall over Othello's
mind. He saw, heard and felt nothing.

Gradually he became aware of
a knocking at the door, and Emilia's
voice calling out, "Murder, my lord!"

Othello stood up stiffly, crossed
the room and opened the door.

"What murder?" he said.

"Roderigo attacked
Cassio, and Cassio
killed him!"
gabbled Emilia.
"Cassio was
wounded, but
he'll live, so—"

Emilia caught
sight of
Desdemona's
body.

"What has happened?"
she squealed.

"I killed her!" Othello
said harshly.

Emilia's screams
attracted Iago and
Montano. Montano
gazed in horror
at Desdemona.

"What's all the screaming
about?" Iago demanded.

"I killed my unfaithful wife," said
Othello. "I found her out when she gave
her handkerchief to her lover, Cassio."

"You're wrong, my lord!" Emilia sobbed.

"Be quiet, woman!" snapped Iago.

"I found the handkerchief yesterday,"
Emilia told Othello. "Iago took it to play
a trick on someone. The trick was played
on you."

Moving faster than a blink, Iago
stepped over to Emilia, stabbed her
through the heart and ran from the
room as she tumbled to the floor. But
he did not get far, for he ran into a troop
of soldiers who had come to arrest him.
Cassio had seen him stab Roderigo, and
had reported it.

Iago was bound with ropes, and marched back into Othello's presence.

Othello looked hard at the man who had deceived him so utterly.

"A trick, Iago?" he said hoarsely. "Are you human, or a devil? If you're a devil, then you can't be killed."

Othello unsheathed his sword and lunged at Iago, who shouted in pain as he jumped back.

A soldier struck the sword from Othello's hand.

Iago laughed scornfully. "I'm bleeding, general, but I'm not dead!" he sneered.

Othello sat on the bed, and took Desdemona's lifeless hands in his own.

"I killed her!" he howled. "I believed Iago's lies and now she's dead. Where am I? Where is the man who used to be Othello?"

Othello reached into his jerkin, brought out a knife and plunged it into his chest. He slumped across Desdemona, and died with his lips touching hers.

"A life for a life, Moor!" Iago said contemptuously.

He did not struggle as the soldiers led him away.

Othello and Desdemona were buried together in the garrison churchyard.

Iago confessed his crimes and was executed. His corpse was burned, and its ashes were scattered on the wind.

I kissed thee ere I killed thee. No way but this:
Killing myself, to die upon a kiss.

Othello; V.ii

Jealousy in Othello

Jealousy and envy are commonly confused, but they are very different. We envy people who have things that we wish we had ourselves: a lovely home, perhaps, or an outstanding talent, such as playing a musical instrument. Jealousy is an obsession, a consuming passion that can take complete control of someone and cause them to twist the meaning of the most innocent words and actions.

Othello is newly married. He has not been in love before, and does not know how jealous love can be. A few words from the vengeful Iago, and Othello begins to doubt Desdemona. Before long, he believes that she has been unfaithful to him with his lieutenant, Cassio. When Othello witnesses Cassio talking about Bianca, he convinces himself that the young man is boasting about his conquest of Desdemona. A flimsy handkerchief seals Desdemona's fate. Othello takes the scrap of cloth as proof of his wife's betrayal. Insane with jealousy, he kills her, and then himself when he discovers her innocence.

Iago, the arch deceiver, is motivated by jealousy and envy. He thinks that Emilia and Othello may have been lovers, and he is resentful that Cassio was promoted to lieutenant instead of him. The revenge he takes is callously cruel.

Othello is unusual among Shakespeare's tragedies. It is not about rulers and the destiny of kingdoms, but concerns itself with a man and his wife in an intimate, almost claustrophobic setting.

It is a drama about human frailty, and a reminder of the destructive power that can be awoken in us all.

Shakespeare and the Globe Theatre

Some of Shakespeare's most famous plays were first performed at the Globe Theatre, which was built on the South Bank of the River Thames in 1599.

Going to the Globe was a different experience from going to the theatre today. The building was roughly circular in shape, but with flat sides: a little like a doughnut crossed with a fifty-pence piece. Because the Globe was an open-air theatre, plays were only put on during daylight hours in spring and summer. People paid a penny to stand in the central space and watch a play, and this part of the audience became known as 'the groundlings' because they stood on the ground. A place in the tiers of seating beneath the thatched roof, where there was a slightly better view and less chance of being rained on, cost extra.

The Elizabethans did not bath very often and the audiences at the Globe were smelly. Fine ladies and gentlemen in the more expensive seats sniffed perfume and bags of sweetly-scented herbs to cover the stink rising from the groundlings.

There were no actresses on the stage; all the female characters in Shakespeare's plays would have been acted by boys, wearing wigs and make-up. Audiences were not well-behaved. People clapped and cheered when their favourite actors came on stage; bad actors were jeered at and sometimes pelted with whatever came to hand.

Most Londoners worked hard to make a living and in their precious free time they liked to be entertained. Shakespeare understood the magic of the theatre so well that today, almost four hundred years after his death, his plays still cast a spell over the thousands of people that go to see them.

Orchard Classics

Shakespeare Stories

RETOLD BY ANDREW MATTHEWS
ILLUSTRATED BY TONY ROSS

Orchard Classics are available from all good bookshops, or can be ordered direct
from the publisher: Orchard Books, PO BOX 29, Douglas IM99 1BQ.
Credit card orders please telephone 01624 836000
or fax 01624 837033 or visit our website: www.wattspub.co.uk
or e-mail: bookshop@enterprise.net for details.

To order please quote title, author and ISBN
and your full name and address.
Cheques and postal orders should be made payable to 'Bookpost plc.'
Postage and packing is FREE within the UK
(overseas customers should add £1.00 per book).

Prices and availability are subject to change.